A Penny Saved

Practical Tips for Money Management

Table of Contents

Chapter 1. Introduction

Title: Special Report - "A Penny Saved: Practical Tips for Money Management"

In today's fast-paced world, navigating your financial landscape can feel like exploring an uncharted territory. But fret not. Our Special Report - "A Penny Saved: Practical Tips for Money Management" - is your trusted handbook, full of simple, easy-to-use strategies for managing your finances. Whether you're a seasoned investor or just starting out, this comprehensive guide with its cheerful, accessible language, is designed to empower you with the knowledge and confidence required to take charge of your financial future. Filled with practical tips, enlightening insights and real-world examples, it's a valuable resource that will help you save more, spend less and navigate towards financial independence. Don't let your money manage you - manage your money. So why wait? Get this special report today and start your journey towards effective money management!

Chapter 2. Understanding Your Financial Landscape

Understanding your financial landscape is an integral initial step towards effective money management. With a clear overview of your current financial situation, you can align your economic decisions and spending habits with your short-term and long-term financial goals.

2.1. Comprehending Your Current Financial Situation

To get started, it is important to assess your current financial situation honestly and meticulously. Consider your income, savings, investments, and debt. Understand the inflow and outflow of your money.

The first aspect of understanding your financial situation is recognizing your source of income. This may include salary from your job, profits from a business, or money received from investments.

The second element to pay attention to is your expenses. These expenses can be classified as fixed and variable expenses. Fixed expenses are those that don't change often over time, such as rent or mortgage payments. Variable expenses, on the other hand, fluctuate, like eating out, groceries, or utilities.

To assess your current financial situation, it is necessary to calculate your net income. This can be done by subtracting your total monthly expenses (both fixed and variable) from your total monthly income.

2.2. Importance of Building an Emergency Fund

An important facet of financial planning is building an emergency fund - a cash buffer to cushion financial hits, such as job loss, major home repairs or sudden medical expenses. Ideally, your emergency fund should contain three to six months' worth of living expenses. This fund should be kept easily accessible, such as in a high-yield savings account or a money market fund.

2.3. The Role of Debt in Your Financial Landscape

Almost every individual carries some form of debt. It could be in the form of student loans, credit card balances, mortgages, car payments or personal loans. While some debt, like mortgages and student loans, can be seen as good debt since they are investments in your future, it is important to manage and reduce high-interest debt, known as bad debt.

To manage debt, start by identifying all of your debts, including the interest rates and repayment terms. From there, it is easier to pinpoint which debts are most pressing and should be paid off first. Creating a debt repayment strategy is essential to gaining control over your debt.

2.4. Navigating the Impact of Taxes

Taxes significantly impact your financial landscape, from your income to your investments. Thus, understanding the tax landscape is crucial. Be aware of the different taxes that you are liable to pay. This can include income tax, sales tax, and property tax among others. Plan your investments and savings in a manner where you can leverage tax benefits to your advantage.

2.5. Considering the Power of Investments

Investments play a significant role in your finances. When done right, investing can help grow your wealth. A smart investment strategy involves diversifying your investments: mix things up with real estate, stocks, bonds and other investment options to spread your risk.

Taking stock of your current financial landscape can be an enlightening experience. It gives you insight into how well you manage your money and where there's room for improvement. From paying off the most troublesome debts, understanding the impact of taxes, to considering investing as a way of increasing wealth, this knowledge can go a long way in leading you towards financial independence.

This process is not an overnight exercise, or a one-time endeavor. Regularly reassessing your finances ensures you remain on track with your goals, and are able to alter your strategies as necessary.

Understanding your financial landscape is a crucial aspect of money management. With this detailed explanation, we hope you are now equipped to assess your own. Your journey towards financial independence begins with a single step. Take it today!

Chapter 3. Setting Smart Financial Goals

Financial goals provide a defined target to aim at, paving the way for diligent financial planning and disciplined spending. Evidently, setting financial goals is the cornerstone of sound financial practices. However, as simple as it sounds, setting effective financial goals requires a clear understanding, strategic planning, and unwavering focus.

3.1. The Importance of Financial Goals

To truly appreciate the process of financial goal setting, it's essential to understand the significance of these goals. Your financial goals represent your monetary aspirations – they may range from short-term objectives like saving for a vacation or buying a new gadget to long-term objectives like saving for your child's education or your retirement.

Having defined financial goals not only offers focus and direction but also provides motivation to stay on top of your savings and investments. They paint a clearer picture of your financial health, by providing clear benchmarks upon which to measure and assess your monetary progress over time. They equip you with a sense of control over your financial decisions and infuse an element of realism into your aspirations by encouraging you to save and invest based on tangible goals rather than vague instincts.

3.2. Identifying Your Financial Goals

Identifying your financial goals is the first step towards smart financial planning. Reflect on what are the short-term, mid-term, and long-term financial goals you want to achieve. Short-term goals are typically under a year, mid-term goals are between one to five years, and long-term goals are over five years. Some of these could be:

1. Short-term: Save for a vacation, buy a new smartphone, pay off small debts.

2. Mid-term: Save for a car or a down payment on a house, pay off larger debts.

3. Long-term: Save for retirement, your children's education, or paying off your house.

Writing your financial goals down will aid in clarity and also serve as a visual reminder, propelling you towards achieving them.

3.3. Making Your Goals SMART

Once you've identified your financial goals, it's time to refine them using the SMART approach. SMART stands for Specific, Measurable, Achievable, Relevant, and Time-bound – an approach that ensures your financial goals are not just dreams but are realistic and achievable.

Specific: Your financial goals need to be clear and well-defined. Vague goals like 'I want to save money' don't provide a clear direction. Instead, being specific such as 'I aim to save $5000 in 2 years for a holiday' gives a definitive goal to work towards.

Measurable: Each goal should be quantifiable; it should state a specific amount that you aim to save or clear off as debt. This way, it's easier to track your progress and take corrective action if needed.

Achievable: Your goals should be realistic and achievable. Placing an unrealistically high savings target within a short span could lead to frustration and demotivation. Break down bigger goals into smaller, attainable milestones.

Relevant: The goal should matter to you and align with your long-term plans. If a goal isn't important to you, it's harder to stay committed to it.

Time-bound: Every goal needs a target date, which creates a sense of urgency and prompts action. Plus, you can calculate how much you need to save each month or year to achieve it.

3.4. Creating a Financial Plan

Now, armed with your SMART goals, you need a concrete financial plan to help turn your goals into reality. Decide a reasonable amount to save from each paycheck, considering your necessary expenses. Analyze your spending habits to uncover hidden spending areas where you can cut back, like unnecessary subscriptions or frequent eating out.

Evaluate appropriate investment vehicles for your longer-term goals. Investing in mutual funds, stocks, bonds, or retirement funds could potentially bring higher returns compared to saving only. However, remember that greater potential return usually comes with more risk. Therefore, understanding risk tolerance and diversifying your investment portfolio is key.

Along the way, make regular reviews of your financial plan a habit to confirm you're on track. Making adjustments is crucial to ensure you stay in line with your financial goals and accommodate changes in your life situation or financial market conditions.

3.5. Overcoming Obstacles

The journey towards your financial goals won't necessarily be a smooth ride; setbacks are inevitable. However, adopting strategies to overcome obstacles can keep you on track. If you're facing a financial crisis, don't completely disregard your savings plan. Instead, try reducing the amount saved. Additionally, create an emergency fund that could cover at least six months of expenses to guard against unforeseen financial disruptions.

Finally, consider seeking professional advice from financial advisors or investing platforms when you need guidance with more complex decision-making.

Financial goal setting is vital to taking control of your finances. The SMART approach coupled with a concrete plan and an attitude to overcome obstacles can put you on a successful path towards achieving your financial goals. After all, a goal without a plan is merely a wish, whereas a goal with a plan becomes an achievement waiting to happen.

Chapter 4. Mastering the Art of Budgeting

The cornerstone of any good financial plan is a sound budget. Budgeting not only assigns purpose to every penny earned but also serves as the lifeline to achieving financial goals. It sketches the path to usher in a life of financial wellness and independence. Yet, budgeting is often regarded as a daunting task, filled with confusion and apprehension. But with an open mind, a dash of determination, and a pinch of persistence, you'll find budgeting to be more of an art than an arduous task. This chapter elucidates the nitty-gritty of crafting an effective budget, offering a holistic approach for anyone yearning to master the art of budgeting.

4.1. Establish Your Financial Goals

First things first. It's essential to know where you're headed. Identifying your financial goals is the initial step in the budgeting process. They act as the lighthouse guiding your financial ship, enabling better decision-making. Goals vary from person to person, but they could be short-term (like planning a holiday), medium-term (like buying a car) or long-term (like retirement planning).

Start by listing down your financial goals in clear terms, assigning realistic time-fractions to each. Once your goals are in place, it's easier to prioritize and strategize your budget accordingly.

4.2. Analyze Income and Expenses

To get started with the budget, you need a detailed account of your income and recurring expenses. Start off by calculating your total monthly income. Include all your income sources like salary, freelance work, dividends, etc. For variable income scenarios, take the average monthly income of the past six months to get a decent estimate.

Next, list out all your expenses. Account for both fixed costs (like rent, groceries, insurance) and variable expenditures (like dining out, hobbies). Create a tracker to record these expenses for a month to get a true sense of your spending patterns. Embrace the power of technology; leverage apps and digital tools that offer tracking and categorizing expenses conveniently.

4.3. Assign Each Dollar a Job

Once you have clear visibility into your income and expenses, allocate specific roles to your dollars. This strategy, commonly known as the zero-based budgeting method, advocates for a purpose for every dollar earned. This could be towards necessities, savings, or payables. The goal is that income minus expenses should equal zero, which means every dollar has been assigned. Balancing this equation provides a realistic picture and prevents overspending, thus facilitating financial control.

4.4. Embrace Essential Budget Categories

Split your spending into essential budget categories. This division makes it easier to track your outflow and adjust in real-time. A popular method is the 50/30/20 rule, where 50% of income serves needs, 30% caters to wants, and the remaining 20% nourishes your savings or debt reduction. Tweaking these proportions according to your situation can lead to a custom budget framework serving your unique financial purpose.

4.5. Monitor, Adjust, Repeat

Budgeting isn't a one-and-done task; it's a continuous process. Financial changes are frequent and unavoidable. A shift in income or an unexpected expense can throw your budget out of balance. However, understanding that adjustments are part of the process is important. A review must be done at least every few months. Adopt a flexible approach and adjust and improve your budget to mirror changes in financial conditions.

4.6. Leverage the Power of Technology

To fine-tune and ease the process of budgeting, leverage the numerous budgeting tools and apps out there. Apps like Mint, YNAB (You Need a Budget), and PocketGuard are great platforms that help you not just create budgets but also monitor and analyze them. These apps automate a lot of your work by linking directly to financial accounts, tracking expenses, and offering helpful insights, thus reaching your financial goals faster.

4.7. Create a Safety Net

It's crucial to incorporate an emergency fund into your budget. The ebb and flow of life often bring with it financial surprises. By setting aside a monthly amount for unplanned expenses, you ensure financial shocks do not disrupt your budget. You'll feel more secure and less stressed knowing that you have contingency funds in place to cover unexpected costs.

4.8. Prioritize Saving and Investing

Saving and investing are crucial aspects of a budget, often neglected for immediate gratification. The trick is to treat these components like a regular expense, i.e., 'paying yourself first.' This practice encourages financial discipline and ensures you're consistently working towards your financial goals. Additionally, it creates a snowball effect, enhancing the growth of your nest egg with the magic of compound interest.

4.9. Plan for Debt Repayment

If you have outstanding debts, including a plan for its repayment is wise. Understand the difference between good debt (usually investments that grow in value) and bad debt (those not increasing in worth, like credit cards). Prioritize clearing bad debts as they can erode your financial health. A systematic repayment strategy in your budget not only lightens the burden but also improves your credit score over time.

Remember, mastering the art of budgeting is not a race but a journey that leads to a financially secure and independent life. Be patient, stay determined, and keep nudging forward. Whether the road is slick or tricky, remember, the power to shape your financial course lies in your hands - or more precisely, in your budget.

Chapter 5. Decoding Banking and Saving Accounts

Banking and saving accounts, the bedrock of personal finance, offer a safe, accessible way to store your money. Understanding how they work is crucial to managing your income efficiently. This chapter will take a deep dive into these accounts, their features, benefits, types, and how to use them wisely.

5.1. The Basics of a Bank Account

A bank account is a financial account maintained by a bank or a similar financial institution where your money is held until you need it. Bank accounts are used to deposit income, withdraw money, pay bills, and save for the future. They provide security, convenience, and easy access to your funds.

Bank accounts are tied to a specific financial institution and identified by an account number. Each is protected up to a specified amount by the Federal Deposit Insurance Corporation (FDIC) in the U.S, or equivalent institutions in other countries. This means if your bank goes under, your money is still safe.

When you open a bank account, the bank will provide you with a checkbook and a debit card. The checkbook can be used for making payments, while the debit card allows you to access your funds electronically.

5.2. Types of Bank Accounts

There are two main types of bank accounts—checking accounts and savings accounts. Each of these has its purpose and features.

5.2.1. Checking Accounts

Checking accounts, also known as transactional accounts, are designed for regular use. You can deposit and withdraw money frequently. These accounts are often used to receive salary payments, pay bills, and heighten day-to-day spending convenience.

Most checking accounts offer unlimited withdrawals. They may also provide check-writing capabilities, online banking options and are usually linked to a debit card. However, checking accounts typically offer lower interest rates compared to other types of accounts.

5.2.2. Savings Accounts

Savings accounts, as the name suggests, are designed to help you save money. They are perfect for stowing away funds you don't intend to spend immediately.

Savings accounts usually offer higher interest rates than checking accounts—this means your money will grow over time. However, due to a rule called Regulation D, you are restricted to six convenient transfers or withdrawals per month.

Other types of bank accounts include money market accounts and certificates of deposit (CDs), which offer higher interest rates, but come with more restrictions.

5.3. Understanding Bank Account Fees

Banks often charge fees, and being aware of these fees can save you from unwanted surprises. Some usual fees associated with a bank account might include:

- Monthly maintenance fee: A charge just for keeping the account open. Some banks will waive this fee if you maintain a certain minimum balance.

- Overdraft fee: Charged when you spend more money than you have in your checking account.

- ATM fee: Associated with using an ATM that belongs to a different bank.

- Transfer fee: Charged for transferring money from one bank to another.

- Insufficient funds fee: Charged when a check is bounced due to insufficient balance in the account.

5.4. The Basics of a Saving Account

A savings account is a deposit account held at a bank or other financial institution that provides principal security and a modest interest yield. As stated earlier, the primary purpose of a saving account is to help you save money while earning interest on your deposits.

5.5. Benefits of a Saving Account

Savings accounts are not just places to keep your money; they offer a range of benefits:

- Security: Your deposits up to a specified limit are insured by the FDIC in the U.S. (or equivalent elsewhere) giving peace of mind that your money is safe.

- Interest income: You earn interest on the money you keep in a saving account.

- Emergency funds: Savings accounts are ideal for setting up an emergency fund to cover unexpected expenses.

- Saving for goals: They can also be used to save for specific goals, like a vacation or a down payment on a home.

5.6. Downsides of a Saving Account

While there are many benefits to saving accounts, they also have their downsides:

- Limited transactions: Typically, you're restricted to six convenient withdrawals or transfers per month.

- Low interest: The interest rates on savings accounts can be lower than those found in other investment vehicles.

- Maintenance fees: Some banks charge fees if you don't maintain a minimum balance in your account.

Understanding the basics of banking and saving accounts is crucial for successful money management. By choosing the right account type based on your needs and being aware of the associated fees, you can efficiently manage your income and grow your savings. Remember, while saving is essential, it's just as necessary to keep these funds where they are safe, accessible, and where they can grow over time.

Chapter 6. Effective Debt Management and Elimination

No one wants to live with the weight of debt looming over them, but poor debt management can lead to this kind of predicament. By understanding the basics of debt management and elimination, we can all steer a clearer path into a more financially secure future.

6.1. Understanding Debt

To start our journey toward effective debt management and elimination, one must first understand what debt is. Debt, in the most basic sense, refers to money owed by one party to another. If you've borrowed money to buy a car, take a vacation, or pay for college - you're in debt. Although not all debt is inherently bad, knowing how to manage it effectively is crucial.

6.2. Good Debt vs Bad Debt

Not all debts are created equal. It's important to separate 'good' debts from 'bad'. Good debt is an investment that will grow in value or generate long-term income. For example, mortgages or student loans can be seen as good debts. On the other hand, bad debt is debt incurred to purchase items that quickly lose their value and do not generate long-term income. Credit card debt is often seen as bad debt because it's often used to purchase depreciating items, like cars or vacations.

6.3. The Importance of Debt Management

Effectively managing your debts is crucial for financial stability. If not properly managed, debts can quickly stack up and jeopardize your financial future. A good debt management plan, however, can help you reduce and eventually eliminate your debts, leaving you financially stable and with a clear path forward.

6.4. Creating a Debt Management Plan

A crucial step in proper debt management is creating a debt management plan. This involves understanding your income and expenses, prioritizing your debts, and figuring out how best to pay them off.

1. Take Stock Of Your Debt: Make a comprehensive list of all your outstanding debts, including the owed amount, the interest rate, the minimum monthly payment, and the due date.

2. Prioritize Your Debt: Not all debts are created equal. Some carry high interest rates, while others may have penalties for early repayment. Prioritize your debts based on interest rates and urgency.

3. Create a Budget: Plan out your monthly spending based on your income and categorize your expenses into "needs" and "wants". This will give you a clear idea of where your money's going and where you can cut back.

6.5. Implementing Your Debt Management Plan

Once you've created your plan, it's time to put it into action. It's vital that you remain committed to your plan, even when things seem tough. Here's how you can stay on track:

1. Limit Your Spending: Resist the urge to spend beyond your

budget. This discipline will help you put more money towards paying off debt.

2. Pay More Than The Minimum: Whenever possible, try to pay more than the minimum amount required on your debt. Even just a little extra can make a significant dent in your overall debt.

3. Create an Emergency Fund: This is a safety net that will help you avoid falling back into debt should unforeseen expenses arise.

4. Reward Yourself: Just because you're on a mission to eliminate debt doesn't mean you can't enjoy life. Learn how to reward yourself on a budget.

6.6. Dealing with Unexpected Setbacks

Reality often wears a different face. Despite meticulous planning, life might throw curveballs. You may lose your job, or an unexpected emergency may drain your finances. Whatever the setback, it's important to adjust your plan to address these changes. Meet with a financial advisor, or a reliable credit counseling agency if necessary. They can help you reassess your financial situation and provide you the guidance needed to navigate through such times.

6.7. The Power of Debt Consolidation

Debt consolidation can be a very effective tool in your debt management strategy. This involves taking out a new loan to pay off multiple debts. The key here is that the new loan should have a lower interest rate than the combined interest rates of your current debts, benefiting you in the long run.

Remember, effective debt management and elimination is not a one-time task, but a way of life. It requires discipline, patience, and perhaps most importantly, a willingness to break away from old financial habits. By implementing these principles and strategies into your daily life, you're one step closer to financial freedom.

Chapter 7. Investing 101: From Basics to Brilliance

Understanding the fundamentals of investing might seem intimidating at first, but armed with the right knowledge and tools, anyone can become a successful investor. Let's start our journey from the basics of investing, and as we climb the ladder of financial mastery, we'll also uncover some brilliant strategies along the way.

7.1. The Basics of Investing

Investing can simply be termed as making your money work for you. This happens when you allow your money to generate more money by putting it into one or several types of investments: stocks, bonds, mutual funds, real estate, or even starting your own business.

Investing is a paramount financial strategy because it allows you to potentially accumulate wealth over time and can serve as a source of income beyond whatever employment you may have. It also helps to protect your money against the eroding effects of inflation.

The world of investing operates on the basic principle of risk and reward: generally, the higher the potential return, the higher the risk of loss. Understanding and managing this balance is crucial to successful investing.

7.2. Types of Investments

There are several types of investments you can make, and each comes with its unique characteristics, risk profile, and potential return. Here are the primary ones:

single

Investment Types: - Stocks - Bonds - Mutual Funds - Real Estate - Exchange-Traded Funds (ETFs)

Stocks allow you to own a piece of a company and share in its profits. Companies issue stock to raise money, and as an investor, you can buy these shares. Owning a stock entitles you to a proportion of the company's earnings and assets.

Bonds are virtually an IOU issued by entities (like corporations and governments) to raise money. As an investor, you lend money to these entities in exchange for regular interest payments and the return of the loan amount when the bond matures.

Mutual Funds are an investment vehicle that pools money from many investors to invest in a diversified portfolio of stocks, bonds, or other assets. Each investor owns shares, which represent a portion of the holdings.

Real Estate involves buying physical property to generate income (through leases, for example) or to sell at a profit.

Exchange-Traded Funds (ETFs) are similar to mutual funds, but they trade on the stock exchange, just like individual stocks.

7.3. Investment Strategies

While there are countless investment strategies, a few basic principles can guide every investor:

- **Diversification**: Spreading your investments across different types of assets can help manage risk. If one investment performs poorly, others may perform well.

- **Dollar-cost averaging (DCA)**: Regularly investing a fixed amount regardless of the market conditions. This can mitigate the risk of making a large investment just before a market downturn.

- **Buy and hold**: Purchasing an investment with the intention to hold on to it for many years. This strategy reduces the impact of short-term volatility.

7.4. Choosing the Right Investment For You

The right investment for you depends on various factors, including your financial goals, risk tolerance, and time horizon. Here are some key points to consider:

- **Goals**: Your investments should align with your objectives. Whether it's buying a house, paying for college, or planning for retirement, different goals require different investment strategies.

- **Risk Tolerance**: This is your ability to withstand losses. If you're unable to sleep at night worrying about your investments, it's a sign that you might be taking on too much risk.

- **Time Horizon**: The length of time you expect to hold an investment before needing the money. The longer your time horizon, the more risk you potentially can take.

7.5. Becoming an Informed Investor

Knowledge is power, and in the world of investing, it can also be the key to wealth. Here are some ways to enhance your financial literacy:

- **Read**: Stay current with news and trends in finance and economics. Read books on investing.

- **Courses and Webinars**: Many institutions offer courses, both online and offline, about investing and finance.

- **Hire a Financial Advisor**: If you're not confident going it alone, hiring a professional advisor is a good option.

Remember, investing is an ongoing journey of learning and growing. As you acquire knowledge and experience, you'll become a more confident and successful investor.

Indeed, the road to investment brilliance begins with understanding the basics. As we continue to navigate through these principles and practices, the path to financial independence will become clearer. Investing is not just about becoming wealthier; it's about securing your future, realizing your dreams, and achieving financial freedom. So take that first step today, because every day is an opportunity in the world of investing.

Chapter 8. Planning for Retirement: It's Never Too Early

Picture a sandy beach under a warm sun, a cozy lakeside cabin, or even a bustling city in another part of the world. For many, visions like these are the heart of retirement dreams. However, achieving this dream requires planning and preparations that start well ahead.

8.1. Why Start Early?

Understanding the importance of early start is the first step to effective retirement planning. Potentially, the younger you start, the smaller the regular investment needs to be to create a significant retirement nest egg. This is because of the power of compound interest, where you not only earn returns on your initial investment but also on the returns that investment has earned over time.

A simple illustration can demonstrate the impact of starting early. Let's consider two individuals, John and Mary. Both invest $200 per month, expect an average annual return of 6%, and plan to retire at 65. The difference is, John starts investing at 25, while Mary begins at 35. By the time they retire, John's investment, thanks to compounding, would have grown to approximately $502,000, while Mary's would only be around $250,000.

As you can see, Mary, despite investing the same total amount as John over a course of 30 years, ended up with significantly less. This example illustrates the substantial leverage that time provides in terms of savings growth.

8.2. Retirement: The Magic Number

Knowing how much you need to save for retirement is one of the biggest challenges when planning for your golden years. The magic number is unique for everyone and depends on various factors such as age, lifestyle, bills, debt, health, and retirement ambitions.

A common rule of thumb is to save at least 70-80% of your pre-retirement income each year during retirement. It typically assumes you'll maintain your current standard of living with some reductions as employment-associated costs will disappear after retirement.

Work out your current expenses and consider how they might change. Some costs, like commuting or professional clothing, will decrease while others, such as travel, hobbies, and healthcare, could increase.

8.3. Building an Investment Portfolio

Building a successful retirement portfolio is more than just saving money, it's about managing and investing it properly. Broadly speaking, your retirement portfolio should focus on equities in the early years when you can afford to take risks, then gradually shift to bonds and fixed income securities as you approach retirement.

The idea is to invest primarily in equities like stocks and mutual funds when young. Though these investments have higher risks in the short term, they typically yield greater return over the long run. A portfolio skewed towards equities in early years can generate substantial growth by the time of retirement.

As you age and retirement approaches, gradually shift investments from equities to bonds and fixed-income securities. These are generally safer and offer steady returns, safeguarding your nest egg from market volatility.

Diversifying your portfolio with different types of investments reduces the risk associated with a single security. To decide on the right asset allocation, consider factors like risk tolerance, time horizon, and financial goals.

8.4. Conscientiously Building Retirement Savings

Once your investment plan is in place, the next crucial step is to create a habit of saving. This can be achieved through various techniques and strategies, like the 'Pay Yourself First' method, which emphasizes routing a specific sum from your salary towards savings before other expenses are met. This ensures that a certain part of your income always goes to savings before it's spent elsewhere.

Automatic transfers to your retirement account can enforce disciplined savings. Also, if your employer offers a 401(k) or a similar retirement plan, and especially if they match your contributions, taking full advantage of this opportunity is a no-brainer. It's essentially free money toward your retirement.

8.5. Pondering Pension and Social Security

While you may likely accumulate most of your retirement funds through savings and investments, do not overlook your Social Security benefits and possibly a pension. There are strategies for maximizing these benefits.

If you're eligible for Social Security, the age at which you begin to collect these benefits can significantly impact your financial health during retirement. While you can start receiving benefits at 62, waiting until your official retirement age or even until you're 70 can result in significantly higher monthly payouts.

Similarly, if you're lucky enough to have a pension plan, understanding how it works will let you incorporate it correctly into your retirement planning. Inquire with your employer about how your pension benefits are calculated, when you can start receiving them, and how they'll be delivered.

8.6. Health Care During Retirement

Healthcare is one of the crucial aspects to consider when planning retirement. Your health condition and the costs associated with it have a significant impact on your retirement savings.

As per studies, an average 65-year-old couple retiring today could expect to spend about $300,000 on healthcare during their retirement. Contributing to a Health Savings Account (HSA), if accessible, can offset these expenses as they grow tax-free and can be withdrawn without penalty for qualified medical costs.

Also, look into long-term care insurance. While not everyone will need long-term care, it has the potential to deplete your retirement savings rapidly if it becomes necessary. Planning for the possibility can save you and your family from financial strain.

8.7. Regular Review

Lastly, regularly reviewing your retirement strategy is not only beneficial, but also essential. Factors like market conditions, lifestyle changes, or alterations in retirement goals can influence your planning. Annual or bi-annual examinations of your retirement portfolio can help keep your plan on the right track.

With these pertinent considerations and tips, it's clear that planning for retirement is not just about setting aside a part of your earnings. It's a comprehensive strategy involving beginning as early as possible, setting realistic retirement goals, building and managing an effective portfolio, securing healthcare, and utilizing available benefits like Social Security and pensions.

Without a doubt, planning for retirement, though complex, needn't be intimidating or cumbersome. It's a process that, when navigated with due diligence and foresight, can ensure that the post-retirement chapter of your life is as fulfilling and rewarding as the years of hard work that led you there.

Chapter 9. Essential Guide to Insurance

Insurance is more than just a financial tool - it's a safety net that helps people protect their financial stability when unexpected events take place. It's about taking charge and preparing for the future. With the following information, our goal is to enable you to have a comprehensive understanding of insurance, helping you make informed decisions that contribute positively to your overall money management strategy.

9.1. Understanding Insurance

Insurance is a contract, or policy, that you purchase from an insurance company to protect yourself or your belongings from financial loss. The agreement involves the insurance company promising to pay for specific losses that might occur in the future in exchange for a regular payment, known as a premium.

There are various types of insurance that cater to different aspects of life, including health, life, auto, homeowner's, long-term care, and pet insurance - the list goes on. The type of insurance to buy depends on one's personal situation and requirements.

9.2. Why Insurance is Necessary

Many may question the necessity of insurance, but its importance cannot be undermined. Insurance provides financial protection against unforeseen events, safeguards income, fosters peace of mind, and is often legally required. It's a financial buffer that ensures that you or your loved ones will not have to shoulder heavy financial burdens during challenging times.

9.3. Types of Insurance

Insurance can broadly be categorized into two groups: personal and business. Personal insurance comprises life insurance, health insurance, automobile insurance, homeowner's insurance, etc. Business insurance, on the other hand, comprises types like liability insurance, worker's compensation, and property insurance etc.

While the myriad of insurance types might seem overwhelming, it's crucial to review each type and determine which one suits your needs best. What works for one person may not necessarily work for another — it's all about personal needs and circumstances.

9.4. How to Choose the Right Insurance

Picking the right insurance requires understanding your needs, assessing potential risks, and considering your budget. Start by identifying what you want to protect, be it your health, life, property, or income. Next, evaluate the potential risks associated with those areas. This step often involves considering the worst-case scenarios and how they could impact you financially.

The final step involves comparing various insurance products based on the coverage they offer and the cost of premiums. It's ideal to select a policy that offers comprehensive coverage at a reasonable cost.

9.5. Insurance Terms You Should Know

Below are some common terms found in insurance policies:

- Premium: This is the amount you pay at regular intervals to keep your insurance policy in force.

- Deductible: The amount you pay out of pocket for losses before the insurance coverage kicks in.

- Claim: A formal request to an insurance company asking for payment based on the terms of the policy.

- Coverage: The degree of protection provided under an insurance policy.

- Policy Limit: The maximum amount an insurer will pay under a policy.

- Exclusions: Situations or conditions the policy won't cover.

- Rider: An amendment to an insurance policy that provides additional coverage or modifies existing coverage.

9.6. Tips for Buying Insurance

Here are some useful tips for purchasing insurance:

- Evaluate Your Needs: Logically assess what kind of insurance you need based on your lifestyle, assets, and liabilities.

- Research: Look into different insurance options, do your due diligence, and seek necessary advice.

- Compare Policies: Don't settle for the first policy you come across. Compare various policies in terms of service, coverage, and price before making a choice.

- Read Terms and Conditions: Understand what is and isn't covered. You should also get clarity about premiums, claim procedures, and any exclusions.

- Re-evaluate Annually: Insurance needs can change over time. Review your coverage once a year to make sure it still fits your needs.

Understanding and navigating the world of insurance can be a daunting task, but it's also an integral part of sound financial planning. With the right knowledge and tools, you can choose the right protection for yourself and your loved ones, safeguarding your financial future against potential risks.

Chapter 10. Navigating Taxes: Keep What's Yours

Paying taxes is an integral part of our financial lives. However, the mechanics of taxation can often be confusing and overwhelming. This chapter aims to break down the complexities of taxes and provide practical tips to help you understand how to optimize and navigate your taxes, allowing you to keep more of what you earn.

10.1. Sub Chapter Heading: Understanding Taxes

To navigate through the labyrinth of taxation, you first need to understand what taxes are and why they matter. Essentially, taxes are mandatory contributions that individuals and businesses make to fund governmental functions. These can range from income to property to goods and services taxes. The key is to familiarize yourself with these tax types and understand how they apply to you.

Income tax, arguably the most well-understood form, is levied on your earnings, including salary, business income, or even gains from investments. Depending upon your location, you may be required to file tax returns annually or at different intervals, outlining your income and relevant deductions to calculate the total tax owed.

Sales tax, on the other hand, is applied to the purchase of goods and services. Buyers typically pay this tax at the point of sale. The tax rate can vary depending on the type of good, locale, and country-specific tax laws.

Property tax, commonly paid by homeowners, is based on the assessed value of your property (land or buildings). Rates and assessment processes can differ substantially from one area to another.

There are other tax types, like payroll tax and excise duties, each with its specific application and rules. Understanding these tax categories is the first step in your journey to successful tax navigation.

10.2. Sub Chapter Heading: Tax Optimization Strategies

Once you have a fundamental understanding of taxes, the next step is adopting strategies to reduce your tax liability legally. Here are several methods you could employ:

- **Tax Deductions**: Tax deductions are specific expenses allowed by tax laws that you can subtract from your gross income to determine your taxable income. They could range from mortgage interest, education expenses, to business expenditures, among others. The deductions available to you depend on your tax jurisdiction's rules. So, make sure you explore and claim all possible deductions for which you are eligible.

- **Tax Credits**: Unlike tax deductions that reduce your taxable income, tax credits reduce your tax liability directly. Examples of tax credits include credits for energy efficiency, education, or raising children. Each tax jurisdiction will have specific credits available to taxpayers, so educate yourself on what is available to you.

- **Investment Shelters**: Certain investment vehicles offer tax advantages, such as retirement accounts or education savings plans. Contributing to these accounts can not only provide you with a saving mechanism but also reduce your taxable income for the current tax year.

- **Tax-Advantaged Investments**: Some investments offer tax benefits such as reduced tax rates on dividends or capital gains, deferral of taxes, or even tax-free withdrawals in retirement. Look for these options when establishing your investment portfolio.

Careful planning can allow you to legally minimize your tax liability and ensure that you retain as much as possible of your hard-earned income.

10.3. Sub Chapter Heading: Tax Planning and Consultation

Another crucial aspect of navigating taxes is planning and consultation. For many people, the complexity of tax laws makes it worthwhile to engage a professional tax preparer or consultant. A tax professional can help you understand the intricacies of the tax code, claim all eligible deductions and credits, and avoid potential issues with the tax authorities.

If you do decide to seek help with your taxes, make sure to choose your tax professional carefully. Look for a certified public accountant (CPA), enrolled agent (EA), or tax attorney who specializes in individual tax returns. It's crucial to remember that even if someone else prepares your returns, you are ultimately responsible for the information provided.

There's no doubt that tax laws can be complex. But by educating yourself, making use of tax-efficient strategies, and seeking professional advice when necessary, you can navigate taxes effectively and keep more of what's yours.

The key to successfully navigating your taxes is knowledge, planning, and utilizing the resources available to you. For a more detailed understanding of your tax situation and effective strategies, consider consulting with a tax professional. The more informed you are, the more likely you are to make decisions that will improve your post-tax bottom line.

Chapter 11. Financial Future-Proofing: Building Wealth Over Time

Building wealth is a journey, not a destination. It takes patience, discipline, and knowledge to develop financial stability. The exciting aspect is that once you comprehend the tactics and strategies necessary, you can start to design a secure financial future and achieve financial independence. Herein lies an exhaustive exploration on how to future-proof your finances by building wealth over time.

11.1. Understanding the Basics of Wealth Building

Before diving deep into strategies, it's crucial to understand the basics related to building wealth. Any wealth-building initiative requires a fundamental understanding of income, expenses, savings, and investments.

Income refers to the money that you earn from various sources such as your job, your side hustle, your business, or your investments. Expenses, on the other hand, are the costs incurred on a regular basis to fund your lifestyle. They typically include rent, bills, groceries, transport, and leisure activities.

The difference between income and expenses is often referred to as savings. Savings serve as a safety net, pad your emergency fund, and provide a resource for investing. This is where the wealth-building journey becomes interesting. Investing involves employing your savings to produce additional income or profits through vehicles such as stocks, bonds, mutual funds, or real estate.

Wealth is built by turning income into savings and then savings into investments. The larger the amount of savings you can invest, and the higher the returns you can generate on these investments, the faster you can accumulate wealth.

11.2. The Power of Compound Interest

Understanding compound interest is pivotal for wealth creation. Compound interest refers to the phenomenon where you earn interest on your original investment and the interest already earned. The power of compound interest stems from 'time'; the longer you allow your investment to grow, the more money you can accumulate.

Here's a simple example of compound interest:

Let's say you invested $10,000 at an interest rate of 5% per year. After a year, your investment grows to $10,500 ($10,000 original investment + $500 interest). In the second year, you start with $10,500, and that earns another 5% interest, equal to $525, making your total investment $11,025. This cycle continues, accumulating more and more wealth because it profits not just from the original investment, but also from the interest accrued in the past.

When it comes to investing for wealth, your best friend is time. The more time you have, the more you can take advantage of compound interest. The most important part is to start as early as possible.

11.3. Embracing a Disciplined Saving Habit

Building wealth necessitates a disciplined approach to saving. Start by living below your means. This doesn't denote a frugal existence; rather, it implies knowing the difference between needs and wants and prioritizing the former. Avoid unnecessary expenses and focus on creating a cushion for yourself.

Implement a budget to align your finances properly. Tracking your income and expenses aids in making informed decisions about where and how your money is spent. Strive to save at least 20% of every paycheck in a separate account tagged for wealth building.

11.4. Diversify Your Investments

Broadening your investment portfolio diminishes the risk associated with investing. Instead of putting all your eggs in one basket, spread your investments across various platforms. Blend your investment portfolio with stocks, bonds, mutual funds, and alternative asset classes to maximize returns and mitigate risk.

Investments differ in terms of risk, reward and time horizon, so what works for someone else may not work for you. Understand your risk tolerance and financial goals before investing your money.

11.5. Take Advantage of Tax-Advantaged Accounts

Tax-advantaged accounts are an excellent tool for wealth building. These accounts come with tax benefits either at the time of investment, during the growth phase, or at the time of withdrawal.

In the U.S, for instance, consider contributing to a 401(k) and an Individual Retirement Account (IRA). These investment vehicles allow your money to grow tax-free until retirement. Similarly, Health Savings Accounts (HSAs) and 529 education savings plans are also tax-advantaged accounts with relevant specific use.

11.6. Consistently Learning and Adapting

The world of finance keeps evolving. As such, continuous learning about new investment vehicles and strategies becomes a staple ingredient for building wealth. Alongside that, be ready to adapt your strategy based on life changes such as job transition, marriage, children, retirement, or unexpected medical expenses.

Furthermore, it's beneficial to seek financial advice from professionals. Working with a financial advisor can help you craft individualized strategies for your financial goals.

Building wealth takes time, but with understanding, discipline, and persistence, it's truly achievable. Stay the course, keep learning, and eventually, you'll have not only wealth but also the peace of mind that financial security brings.

www.ingramcontent.com/pod-product-compliance
Lightning Source LLC
Chambersburg PA
CBHW071011260726
48661CB00007B/2908